tropical cocktails

for the MODERN BAR

TIKI

DRINKS

NICOLE WESTON and ROBERT SHARP

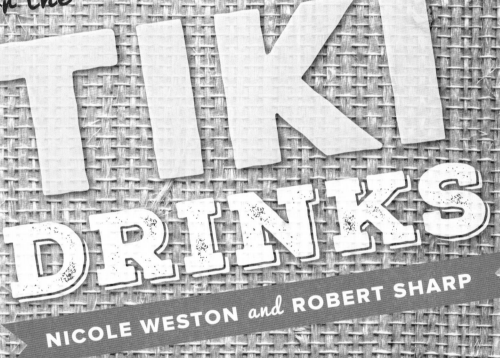

Tropical cocktails

for the MODERN BAR

TIKI DRINKS

NICOLE WESTON and ROBERT SHARP

THE COUNTRYMAN PRESS, WOODSTOCK, N.Y.

Tiki Drinks Photo Credits:

All photography by Robert Sharp.
Illustrations as credited below:

Page 1, 37, 138: © patty_c/iStockphoto.com; 2, 3, 50, 89, 142: © billnoll/iStockphoto.com; 4, 31, 32, 39, 52, 63, 79, 95: © kanyakits/iStockphoto.com, © sundarananda/iStockphoto.com; 24, 35, 44, 55, 84, 88, 116, 131, 140, 144, 153: © locotearts/iStockphoto.com; 25: © DNY59/iStockphoto.com; © sundarananda/iStockphoto.com, © Graffizone/iStockphoto.com; 26, 65, 105: © LOVE_LIFE/iStockphoto.com; 27, 103, 115: © Graffizone/iStockphoto.com, © bullantmultimedia/iStockphoto.com; 28, 64, 87, 92, 100, 124, 136: © locotearts/iStockphoto.com, © KarolinaL/iStockphoto.com; 29, 110: © SalomeNJ/iStock.com; 33, 41, 57, 73, 77, 85, 97, 102, 129, 137: © daikokuebisu/iStockphoto.com; 34, 54, 78, 121, 134: © daikokuebisu/iStockphoto.com, © Llepod/iStockphoto.com; 36, 128: © KarolinaL/iStockphoto.com, © ipopba/iStockphoto.com; 40, 68, 108: © magenetcreative/iStockphoto.com, kanyakits/iStockphoto.com; 43, 48: © KarolinaL/iStockphoto.com, © locotearts/iStockphoto.com; 45, 69, 109: © melazerk/iStockphoto.com; 46, 70, 126: © mashuk/iStockphoto.com; 47, 83: © CSA-Printstock/iStockphoto.com; 51, 91, 112: © Graffizone/iStockphoto.com; 56: © sundarananda/iStockphoto.com, © locotearts/iStockphoto.com, © kanyakits/iStockphoto.com; 59, 71, 72, 76, 107, 123, 127, 139: © kanyakits/iStockphoto.com, © sundarananda/iStockphoto.com, © Graffizone/iStockphoto.com; 60, 132, 148: © sundarananda/iStockphoto.com, © locotearts/iStockphoto.com; 61, 133, 149: © sundarananda/iStockphoto.com, © DNY59/iStockphoto.com, © Graffizone/iStockphoto.com; 66, 86, 118: © patty_c/iStockphoto.com, © Llepod/iStockphoto.com; 67: © Barcin/iStockphoto.com; 75, 80, 96, 104, 111, 120, 147: © KarolinaL/iStockphoto.com, © Graffizone/iStockphoto.com; 81, 101, 117: © DNY59/iStockphoto.com; 90: © mashuk/iStockphoto.com; 93, 125, 141: © SalomeNJ/iStock.com, © Llepod/iStockphoto.com; 99, 135, 143: © CSA-Printstock/iStockphoto.com, © Graffizone/iStockphoto.com; 113: © billnoll/iStockphoto.com; © mashuk/iStockphoto.com; 119: © Kanyakits/iStockphoto.com, © Graffizone/iStockphoto.com; 146: © mashuk/iStockphoto.com, © daikokuebisu/iStockphoto.com

Page texture: © tomograf/iStockphoto.com

The Countryman Press
Woodstock, Vermont
www.countrymanpress.com

A division of W. W. Norton & Company, Inc.
500 Fifth Avenue, New York, NY 10110
www.wwnorton.com

For information about special discounts for bulk purchases, please contact W. W. Norton Special Sales at specialsales@wwnorton.com or 800-233-4830

All photos by the author unless otherwise noted.

Printed in the United States
Design by LeAnna Weller Smith

Library of Congress Cataloging-in-Publication Data

Weston, Nicole.
 Tiki drinks : tropical cocktails for the modern bar / Nicole Weston and Robert Sharp.
    pages cm
 Includes index.
 ISBN 978-1-58157-302-2 (hardcover)
 1. Cocktails. I. Sharp, Robert (Mixologist) II. Title.

 TX951.W428 2015
 641.87'4—dc23

                    2015006644

 10 9 8 7 6 5 4 3 2 1

DEDICATED TO EVERYONE WHO KNOWS
WHERE THE RUM HAS GONE

CONTENTS

INTRODUCTION

Many people think of tiki drinks as being extremely fruity and syrupy-sweet, but that idea of a tiki drink is from the decline of the tiki trend, when drink mixes, not fresh fruit juices, were the standard behind the bar. When the first mixologists started to make the first tiki drinks, they were made with fresh juices, high-quality rums, and homemade sweeteners—not just because these ingredients make for a better cocktail, but because the tiki drinks that they were creating were like nothing anyone had ever tasted before.

As tiki drinks regain popularity, they need an ingredient-driven, craft cocktail–style makeover to give a new generation of cocktail drinkers an appreciation of what the original craze was about.

A HISTORY OF TIKI

The idea of a tiki drink probably conjures up images of kitschy 1970s bars serving brightly colored, syrupy-sweet blended drinks in tall, curving glasses. Tiki was definitely popular in the 1970s, but tiki drinks have been around much, much longer than that.

The first tiki bar was Don's Beachcomber Cafe, which opened in Los Angeles in 1934, shortly after Prohibition was repealed. During Prohibition, rum was a popular spirit because it was easily smuggled into the United States from the Caribbean, where it was produced. After the repeal of the 18th Amendment, bar patrons could go back to drinking whiskey and gin, spirits they had not had in quite some time, and rum became extremely cheap. An enterprising and well-traveled man named Donn Beach—born Ernest Raymond Beaumont Gantt—decided to take advantage of all that inexpensive rum and turn it into something completely different.

Inspired by his travels through the Caribbean and the South Pacific, he opened Don's Beachcomber Cafe—later renamed Don the Beachcomber—as a Polynesian-themed restaurant serving up tropical drinks and exotic food that you couldn't find anywhere else.

The restaurant was a huge hit with Hollywood celebrities and you could find such people as the Marx Brothers and Clark Gable dining there on any given night. But while these patrons were the stars of the silver screen, the cocktails were the stars at Don the Beachcomber. The drinks were unlike anything you would find at any other bar. They used lots of citrus and tropical fruit juices, a wide variety of rums—some blended together to create completely new flavor profiles, and house-made syrups and liqueurs that added additional layers of flavor. The drinks used secret recipes that Donn himself came up with; they were so secret that even

the bartenders didn't know exactly what went into the bottles that they used to mix such drinks as the Zombie and the Vicious Virgin.

Don the Beachcomber might have been a one-off themed bar instead of the start of an enduring trend if it wasn't for Victor Bergeron, better known as Trader Vic, who owned a bar in Oakland, California, called Hinky Dinks. Perhaps inspired by the success of Don the Beachcomber in Hollywood, he transformed his bar into a Polynesian paradise and relaunched it in 1937 as Trader Vic's. Trader Vic was a shrewd businessman and it wasn't long before Trader Vic's franchises began to open. The first was in Seattle in 1940 and they spread all over the globe from there. More than a dozen locations still operate today.

As popular as these early tiki bars were, the tiki craze didn't really take off until after World War II ended. In the late 1940s, thousands of American servicemen were returning from time spent in the South Pacific and Hawaii with a bit of a taste for exotic fruits, juices and foods. At the same time, air travel to those places—particularly to Hawaii—was becoming both very affordable and very popular. The middle class was inspired by the food, drink, and flair of all things exotic. This new taste for Polynesian Pop culture led to the opening of hundreds of tiki bars all across the country, giving everyone access to that romanticized Hawaiian vacation without ever needing to head to the airport.

The first wave of tiki culture began to crest in the mid-1960s and came crashing down in the 1970s. Bars were serving syrupy-sweet drinks made from premade mixes, not from fresh fruit, and much of the original exoticism had worn off. Many of the original tiki bars had closed down—the original Trader Vic's closed in 1972—and all tiki-philes were left with was a handful of small bars that tenaciously clung to their old recipes and loyal clientele.

Today, tiki cocktails are seeing a major revival for the first time in decades. Tiki drinks are once again being made with fresh juices, homemade syrups, and high-quality rums. Classic drinks are being served by bartenders who are rediscovering old recipes and new tiki drinks are being innovated by cocktail enthusiasts who are learning just how delicious rum really is.

The recipes in this book are meant to bring both classic and modern tiki drinks to life. They capture those exotic flavors that made tiki culture such a huge hit in its heyday, but in a way that is balanced and designed to appeal to the modern palate. This isn't to say that we're taking these drinks too seriously. In addition to being delicious, tiki drinks should be a lot of fun, and we can guarantee that you're going to have a lot of fun as you drink your way through these cocktails.

INGREDIENTS

RUM

Rum is the most important ingredient in the bar for a tiki mixologist and it is what really sets tiki drinks apart from most other cocktails. Rums are generally produced in tropical countries that also produce sugar, since they are made from sugarcane, molasses, and other by-products of the sugar production process. Even though rums are made with the same basic ingredient, they can taste very different depending on their place of origin.

Rum, like wine, has a strong sense of terroir, which means that rums from different rum-producing countries have very different flavor profiles. This means that one rum can taste very different from another and switching out the basic rum in a cocktail can completely change the flavor of the drink. That said, we know that you don't have to pick up two dozen different brands of rum that you've never heard of before you even try any of the cocktails in this book. Instead of giving you a shopping list, we're giving you a crash course in rum that will let you know what to expect before you buy a bottle. The rums that we use in our recipes are categorized fairly broadly, so you can use what you already have with a little more flexibility. That said, the particular type of rum matters more in some drinks than others and, when it does, we always note that in the recipe.

The bottom line: You will get the best results in your cocktails if you use high-quality rums in these recipes. Not unlike wine, rums that cost a little bit more tend to taste a whole lot better. This doesn't necessarily mean that you always have to use top-shelf spirits in your cocktails, but we really recommend avoiding the bottom shelf unless you're going to be making drinks for people you want to leave the party quickly.

RUMS BY TYPE

Rum is made from fresh-pressed sugarcane juice, cane sugar, or molasses and other by-products of cane sugar production. The sugar mixture is fermented, then distilled before it is ready to drink. At this point, the rum can be bottled or aged in barrels. Unlike vodka, rum is almost never filtered, because that process removes the unique flavors that rum makers try to bring out in their spirits.

White or light rums are unaged and tend to have a dry, subtle flavor when compared to aged rums, though there is a big difference between the flavor found in inexpensive and expensive unaged rums. Although many people tend to reach for these as a standard mixed-drink rum, you would miss out on a lot of potential flavor by relying on them as your primary type of rum.

Aged or gold rums are rums aged in oak barrels and have greater depth of flavor than

white rums do. The oak barrels are typically previously used bourbon barrels. These barrels are charred on the inside and infuse the rum with color, but have been used long enough that the rum doesn't usually take on a charred flavor the way that whiskey aged in a new barrel will. Rums that are aged longer will have a darker color. Rums can be aged anywhere from three years to more than two decades and there are many reasonably priced options. The rums at the upper end of the spectrum are quite expensive and meant for sipping, though they can make a memorable cocktail if you feel like treating yourself.

Dark rums are typically made from molasses or some sort of caramelized cane juice and are aged in oak barrels. The aging varies from brand to brand, and dark rums are frequently made of a blend of shorter- and longer-aged rums. They retain some of the residual molasses in the finished product, giving them an intense flavor and a thicker consistency than white or gold rums.

Rhum agricole is a style of rum that is made exclusively from fresh sugarcane juice, rather than from molasses or other sugar by-products. This style of rum originated in the French Caribbean around the turn of the nineteenth century, when beet sugar became popular in Europe and sugarcane farmers were left with a surplus of sugarcane. Rum distillers opted to ferment the juice directly into rum and the result was rhum agricole. It has velvety texture and a smooth, vegetal, grassy flavor that is very different from molasses-based rums. The best-known rhums agricoles come from Martinique and are labeled "AOC Rhum Agricole Martinique," which means that there are certain defined standards for production of rhum at the island's dozen or so distilleries. Rhum agricole can be white and unaged or aged in oak barrels to give it whiskey-like qualities.

Overproof rum is bottled with a higher alcohol content than standard rums (about 40% ABV). A rum can be considered overproof if it is greater than 100 proof (50% ABV); however the most well-known overproof rums are 151 proof (75% ABV). Extremely high-proof rums are very flammable and are often floated on top of drinks and lit on fire for an eye-catching drink presentation.

Flavored and spiced rums have sweeteners and other flavorings added to them. They can also contain additional colorings. Flavored rums often feature tropical fruits that you can infuse into cocktails using the fruits themselves, while spiced rums can have more unusual flavor profiles and can bring a little more complexity to a cocktail.

RUMS BY COUNTRY

Barbados—Barbados has a long history of rum production, mostly because that is where large-scale sugarcane production originally took off, and its rums are known for being aromatic and sweet, with a distinct sweetness and pronounced fruit flavors, but less of the extreme tropical fruitiness of Jamaican rums. Popular brands: Mount Gay, Foursquare, Doorly's.

Brazil—The Brazilian spirit cachaça is not called rum, but it is distilled from sugarcane juice in a process that is very similar to that of rhum agricole. Like other rums, cachaça is sold both unaged and aged; however, the white varieties are more often used in cocktails and are, as a result, much more widely available. Popular brands: Leblon, Cachaça 51, Pitú.

Guyana—Rum from Guyana is known as Demerara rum, because the Demerara River region of Guyana has long been noted for its fine rums. Demeraras have some of the same overripe tropical fruit flavors that you'll find in Jamaican rums, but tend to come with a bit more subtlety of flavor. Popular brands: El Dorado, Pyrat, Skipper.

Jamaica—Jamaican rums are known for being rich, funky, and sweet, with a strong flavor of overripe bananas, tropical fruits, and molasses, regardless of what brand of rum you are drinking. These full-bodied rums lend a lot of flavor to a cocktail. Popular brands: Appleton Estate, Smith & Cross, Myers's, Wray & Nephew.

Martinique—Rum produced in Martinique is known as rhum agricole and it is made only from pressed sugarcane juice, not molasses. Rhum agricole has distinct grassy, vegetal flavors that you don't typically find in other rums, making it a unique ingredient for which there really is no substitute. Agricole-style rums are made in other places, but the rums from Martinique are the best known. Popular brands: Clément and Rhum JM.

Puerto Rico—Puerto Rican rums are known for being light bodied with a subtle flavor. This can make them a good choice for punches and other juice-heavy drinks, where you are not getting a lot of flavor directly from the rum, but they won't have the same impact in a rum-forward cocktail. Cuban rums are made in a similar style, though they are not as widely available. Popular brand: Bacardi.

Trinidad—Trinidad is a relatively small producer of rums, but its rums are always memorable. Trinidad rums are best known for their rich caramel sweetness and distinct vanilla notes, which makes them very approachable as both mixing and sipping rums. Popular brands: Zaya, 10 Cane, Scarlet Ibis, Angostura.

JUICES

Fresh juices are one of the hallmarks of good tiki drinks and we try to work with fresh juice whenever possible. This is particularly important when it comes to citrus. When it is freshly squeezed, citrus always has a bold, zesty flavor, whether you are juicing a sweet orange or a tart lime. As it sits out, citrus juice becomes gradually more bitter. To try to counteract this, many commercial juice producers need to add sugar to try to balance that bitterness. The result is a citrus juice that is bland and lacks the punch of freshly squeezed juice. Every one of these drinks will taste better if you squeeze the lemons, limes, and oranges as you go. The bonus is that you will have plenty of citrus rind on hand to use for garnish!

When it comes to other juices, such as pineapple or guava, it may not be possible or practical to juice your own fruit. In this case, look for commercially available juices that don't have sugar or corn syrup added to them. You can control the sweetness of your cocktails by adding additional syrups if necessary, but you can't take it out of the juice if you buy it that way.

COCONUT

Coconut is probably one of the first flavors that comes to mind when you think about tropical drinks and we incorporate it in many recipes. We use both cream of coconut and coconut water in our recipes.

Coconut water is the clear liquid that you find in the center of a fresh coconut when you crack it open. It has a subtle coconut flavor and a natural sweetness.

Cream of coconut is coconut milk that has been sweetened and thickened, much the same way that sweetened condensed milk is made from regular milk. It is a great ingredient to work with when making drinks because it gives cocktails a lovely color and consistency, as well as a good coconut flavor.

There are no good substitutes for coconut water or cream of coconut. Coconut milk, for instance, is not thick enough or sweet enough to substitute for cream of coconut, and it is too thick to substitute for coconut water. Fortunately, coconut water is readily available in most grocery stores—no coconut needed. Cream of coconut is readily available at most liquor stores. Coco López is the most well-known brand and will work very well in all of our recipes.

SYRUPS AND SWEETENERS

People often protest that they don't like sweet drinks before drinking—and enjoying—a well-balanced tiki drink. Tiki drinks aren't necessarily sweet, but sweeteners and syrups do play an important role in building them.

Sugar has long been an important cocktail ingredient, as its sweetness helps disguise the burn of alcohol in even the simplest drinks. Sugar balances the acid in tart citrus and brings out the sweet flavors of tropical fruit and vanilla that pop up in so many rums. Sugar and sugar syrups should make cocktails taste better and more balanced, not just sweeter.

We make our own sugar syrups and recommend that you do the same, largely because it is so easy and so inexpensive to make them yourself. It is also easy to customize the flavors to suit your own tastes. Our Spiced Simple Syrup (page 150) is a great example of this, and it is a recipe to which you could easily add other spices to give it a unique flavor. That said, you can easily buy commercial versions of most basic syrups and they are worth keeping in your bar if you don't want to take the time to make your own.

ICE

Ice is just as important to tiki drinks as rum is and you should be very generous with your ice. Not only does it make a drink refreshingly cold, but a little bit of water can really bring out the flavors of a cocktail. Classic tiki drinks were almost always served in a glass filled with crushed ice and so are most of our recipes. Crushed ice has a lot of surface area, which means that it will chill your drink much faster than any regular ice cube will. Because the drink cools down so rapidly, you won't have much ice melting after the first minute or so, and unless you are a very slow sipper, your drink should stay just as tasty from start to finish.

If you have a refrigerator that makes crushed ice, you should have no problem making any drink in this book. If you don't, you're going to need to crush the ice by hand. You can do this by placing whole ice in a resealable plastic bag, a canvas bag, or a clean dish towel and hitting it with a small mallet or rolling pin. The process is almost as therapeutic as sipping a finished cocktail, even though it can get a bit noisy!

Because crushed ice takes up much more space in a glass than cubed ice does, you will need more ice than you expect when you are entertaining. If you know you're going to be serving a lot of drinks, set your ice maker on high a few days in advance or pick up some large bags of commercial ice to use so that you have enough on hand.

BAR TOOLS

It is easy to make great cocktails when you are starting out with the right equipment. A few essential tools will make your life very easy.

Shaker There are two types of shapers: a Boston shaker and a standard shaker. The Boston shaker is the style that is used by most professionals and has a metal shaker and a tempered glass mixing glass that fit together snugly. To use one of these, you will need a separate strainer to hold back the ice while you pour out your cocktail. The standard shaker typically has a strainer built into the top and is generally easier to use. Either style will get the job done nicely.

Bar spoon A bar spoon is a very long-handled spoon that is ideal for stirring the ingredients in a "built" cocktail. The spoon is also a teaspoon measure, which makes it a convenient option for measuring out small quantities of liquors or other liquids.

Measuring glass A measuring glass or a jigger will help ensure that your pours are consistently accurate as you build your cocktails. While very experienced bartenders can free-pour their spirits for many drinks, tiki cocktails tend to involve lots of ingredients in relatively small quantities. A measuring glass is the only way to ensure that your drinks are accurately measured and will come out tasting exactly the same time after time. We prefer to use measuring glasses, not jiggers, so that no guesswork is involved when measuring out small amounts.

Juicer A juicer is an essential component of a tiki mixologist's bar. Fortunately, a handheld citrus press is inexpensive and extremely efficient, so you don't need to splurge on an expensive electric juicer to make great drinks.

Blender A good blender will crush ice to a fine, even consistency each and every time. It is good to have a blender with multiple speeds, as the low speeds are good for coarsely crushing ice, while the higher speeds are best for blending an icy drink to a smooth consistency. More expensive blenders tend to perform better than inexpensive ones, so it is worth splurging on a good blender if you have a soft spot for creamy blended cocktails. That said, if you have an expensive blender, you might find that you start to enjoy blended cocktails a whole lot more.

BAR TECHNIQUES

Bartending is an art—and if you don't feel that way, you'll certainly start to after you've mixed up a few dozen cocktails. It looks easier than it is, but a few simple techniques are all you need to get the basics down.

Batching When you need to serve a crowd, you might find that you need to double or triple a recipe. This process is called batching. Some of our drink recipes are for bowls designed to serve more than one person and the blended drink recipes can all easily be scaled up. As a general rule, however, it is best to make these drinks one serving at a time to ensure that they are balanced and consistently delicious, as some drinks use strongly flavored ingredients, such as Allspice Dram (page 153), which should not necessarily be doubled when batching.

Blending To make the smoothest possible drink in a blender, all of the liquids should be added first, followed by the ice. The blender should be started at a low speed, to crush the ice, then the speed should be increased to HIGH to completely pulverize the ice and produce a smooth, creamy drink.

Building Built drinks are not shaken; the ingredients are simply stirred together with long-handled bar spoon. Drinks that use carbonated components, such as sparkling wine or ginger beer, are usually built.

Floating A float is a small amount of liquid, often a liqueur, which is poured on top of a cocktail to add a final layer of flavor. Drizzle the additional liquid in over the back of a bar spoon held just over the surface of a cocktail.

Muddling Muddling is the process of crushing ingredients together at the bottom of a glass. A special tool, called a muddle, usually made out of wood, is designed just for this purpose. When muddling, you should press your ingredients—usually mint leaves or fruit—firmly, twisting the muddle as you work to release their flavors without pureeing them.

Shaking Most of these cocktails are shaken drinks. To make a shaken drink, combine the ingredients in a mixing glass or the base of a shaker, add a generous scoop of ice, and put on the lid. Shake vigorously for at least 20 seconds, until the shaker is ice cold, then strain the contents of the drink through a strainer into your waiting glass.

Swizzling Swizzling is the process of stirring a drink with a swizzle stick. A swizzle stick is a long stick with four or five short prongs on one end. The pronged end is inserted into an ice-filled drink and the long end is rolled quickly between the palms of your hands, creating a motion that swirls the ice, quickly chilling the drink and causing a layer of frost to build up on the sides of the glass. You can buy a plastic swizzle stick, but the authentic swizzle sticks actually come from a plant in the Caribbean that produces branches ideal for swizzling. If you don't have a swizzle stick, a long-handed bar spoon can also get the job done.

GLASSWARE AND GARNISHES

Tiki drinks are known for their fancy mugs and over-the-top garnishes, but you don't need to go crazy to showcase a drink that is delicious on its own.

GLASSWARE

There are several basic types of glasses that you will need to have in your bar as you make these drinks.

Coupe/Martini These small glasses are used for drinks that are served without ice. It's not typical of a tiki drink to be served without ice, but several of our new classics are best enjoyed that way.

Goblet This is a bowl-like, wide-mouthed, stemmed glass that is similar in appearance to a large wineglass. Goblets generally hold 12 to 16 ounces and are ideal when you want extra room for a particularly large or creative garnish.

Highball/Collins Collins glasses are tall, straight-sided glasses designed for holding long drinks. A highball glass is tall, but the shape of the glass varies much more than does the shape of a collins glass. Both types of glasses hold approximately the same amount of liquid, about 10 ounces.

Hurricane This is a tall, hourglass-shaped glass that holds from 16 to 20 ounces. It is most often used with blended cocktails, but it can be used for any large drink. As you won't see a glass like this in a "regular" bar, it will instantly add a little fun to any drink you serve in it.

Poco Grande This hourglass-shaped glass has a smaller, stouter bowl than a hurricane does, with a much longer stem. It typically holds about 12 ounces and is a good choice for drinks that can't quite fill up a standard hurricane.

Rocks/Old-Fashioned A rocks glass is the most versatile glass you have. Technically there are both single and double old-fashioned glasses; however, it is becoming less and less common to see the single rocks glasses, in favor of the larger ones. Larger rocks glasses typically hold from 10 to 14 ounces, though because the glasses will be filled with crushed ice before you add your cocktail, your drink won't be quite that large.

Tiki mugs Funky, colorful tiki mugs are available as souvenirs from your favorite local tiki bars and online from retailers that specialize in kitsch. They are a great way to serve your cocktails, though you won't get to enjoy the color of the cocktail the same way that you will in traditional glassware. Most tiki mugs are quite large and you might find that you need to double a drink recipe to fill the glass all the way up. If using a tiki mug, you don't really need much garnish because the mug will attract enough attention on its own.

GARNISHES

You can have a lot of fun with the garnish when it comes to tiki drinks. You can use almost anything you can think of, from a simple maraschino cherry to a plastic toy pirate, to finish your drink off in a fun, eye-catching way. If you can, however, it is always a good idea to match the garnish to the drink, because a garnish can lend one final aroma to the drink before it is served and that can take the cocktail experience from good to great.

Citrus—Citrus is our go-to garnish because it is so versatile. Almost every drink uses some kind of citrus, which makes it easy to choose whether you should use lime, lemon, or orange to garnish your drink. You can cut the fruit into triangular wedges or circular rounds or use a peeler to remove a twist from the citrus skin. If you're feeling creative and have a sharp knife, you can cut a large slice of citrus peel—with the flesh of the fruit removed—into a shape, such as a skull or rocket ship.

Other fruit—Pineapple wedges are always a popular garnish for tiki drinks because this fruit instantly conveys a tropical feeling. Whole pineapple is the best choice for garnish because the whole fruit has much more structural integrity than canned pineapple rings do. To secure your wedge on the rim of your glass, simply cut a small slit in the side and ease the pineapple into place.

Star fruit, melons, and berries all make easy, colorful garnishes. Smaller fruits, such as cherries, are best secured with cocktail picks to hold them in place.

Mint—Mint has always paired well with rum, and while not every drink is going to use mint as a flavor, mint has been a staple tiki garnish since the creation of the original Mai Tai. A fresh sprig of mint gives a great pop of color to a cocktail and is a great, low-maintenance garnish option.

Flowers—Dendrobium orchids are the most commonly used flower for garnishing cocktails and they are available at many florists. The orchids themselves are edible, but are never intended to be eaten along with your drink. They are there for looks alone. In addition to orchids, other edible flowers, including carnations, roses, and hibiscus, also make attractive drink garnishes. Try to buy organically grown flowers that are free from pesticides. Even if you aren't going to be eating your garnish, it is best to keep chemicals away from your cocktails.

Umbrellas and cocktail picks—Umbrellas add a splash of color that cocktail picks alone don't, but both of these pointy drink accessories are useful for finishing a drink because they can skewer such items as cherries and pineapple wedges together. It's always easier to handle your garnishes if they come in one piece, rather than in many small pieces. For a more tiki look, keep an eye out for knotted bamboo cocktail picks, rather than regular toothpicks.

Cocktail straws—These short, thin straws that are designed just for cocktails. Unlike regular straws, cocktail straws are so narrow that ice won't get stuck in them as you sip, which makes drinking much easier. They're usually added to drinks in pairs and not used alone.

aku aku

MAKES 1

The Aku Aku is a cocktail that will taste much more familiar than it sounds. This refreshing minty cocktail is reminiscent of a mojito, but with a more subtle sweetness and a bit more complexity. The fresh mint leaves are shaken with the rest of the ingredients as the drink is prepared, but they are not strained out, which gives the drink an unusually colorful look.

1 ounce white rum

2 ounces apricot brandy

1 ounce lime juice

½ ounce pineapple juice

¼ ounce Simple Syrup (page 150)

10 large mint leaves

Combine all the ingredients, including the mint leaves, in a shaker and fill with crushed ice. Shake vigorously for 20 to 30 seconds, until very cold. Pour the contents of the shaker into a goblet.

chief lapu lapu

MAKES 1

The Chief Lapu Lapu is a fruit-forward drink named after a Filipino chief from the 1500s. With a blend of orange, lemon, and passion fruit juices, this drink has little to do with an ancient warrior, but you can still raise a toast to him when you pick up your glass.

¾ ounce white rum

¾ ounce dark rum

1½ ounces orange juice

1 ounce lime juice

½ ounce passion fruit puree

½ ounce Simple Syrup (page 150)

Combine all the ingredients in a shaker and fill with ice cubes. Shake vigorously for 20 to 30 seconds, until very cold. Strain the contents of the shaker into a rocks glass filled with crushed ice and serve.

cobra's fang

Tiki drinks often have a bit of a bite to them, as the blend of tropical fruit juices used to build the drinks is useful for hiding an extra splash of rum. The Cobra's Fang, a recipe originally created by Don the Beachcomber, is easy to drink and delivers a surprising bite at the end. It's a complex drink, with a blend of lime and orange and a hint of cherry and spice.

1½ ounces aged rum

¾ ounce overproof rum

½ ounce lime juice

½ ounce orange juice

½ ounce Falernum (page 132)

½ ounce Spiced Simple Syrup (page 150)

¼ ounce *Luxardo* maraschino liqueur

Combine all the ingredients in a shaker and fill with ice cubes. Shake vigorously for 20 to 30 seconds, until very cold. Strain the contents of the shaker into a rocks glass filled with crushed ice. Garnish with a cobra (see note) and serve.

How to Make a Cobra Garnish

Use a vegetable peeler to remove a wide strip of peel from an orange. Use a small knife to cut one end of the peel into a diamond shape, to resemble a snake's head. Add two whole cloves to the snake's head, to serve as eyes.

dark & stormy

MAKES 1

This two-tone cocktail is a Bermudan staple that is always made with Goslings Black Seal rum and ginger beer. The Goslings has a distinctively dark color and a smoky flavor that offers a contrast in both looks and flavor to sweet, spicy ginger beer, and we recommend sticking to that rum for the best results in the drink. The original recipe is limited to two ingredients; our version includes a bit of lemon and lime to make the spice of the ginger beer pop even more.

1½ ounces Gosling's Black Seal rum

½ ounce lemon juice

½ ounce lime juice

Ginger beer

Fill a highball glass with ice. Add the rum, lemon juice, and lime juice. Top with ginger beer and stir with a bar spoon to combine the ingredients. Garnish with a citrus ship (see note).

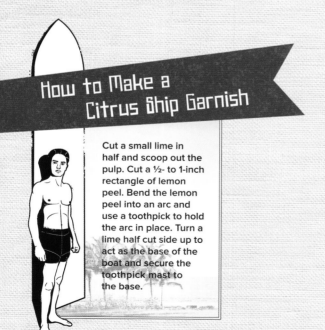

How to Make a Citrus Ship Garnish

Cut a small lime in half and scoop out the pulp. Cut a ½- to 1-inch rectangle of lemon peel. Bend the lemon peel into an arc and use a toothpick to hold the arc in place. Turn a lime half cut side up to act as the base of the boat and secure the toothpick mast to the base.

eastern sour

MAKES 1

The Eastern Sour is a tiki twist on a whiskey sour that was invented by Trader Vic in honor of the first Trader Vic's to open in Toronto, a city that may have been better known for favoring whiskey than rum at the time. We like to use an oaky bourbon in this spiced-up version of the original drink.

1½ ounces bourbon

½ ounce Allspice Dram (page 153)

¼ ounce lime juice

¼ ounce Simple Syrup (page 150)

Combine all the ingredients in a shaker and fill with ice cubes. Shake vigorously for 20 to 30 seconds, until very cold. Strain the contents of the shaker into a rocks glass filled with crushed ice and serve.

fog cutter

MAKES 1

While many tiki drinks use just one type of spirit as a base, the Fog Cutter uses three: rum, bourbon, and gin. Each element lends something unique to the cocktail, and you end up with a drink that has a hint of molasses, a bit of vanilla, and some refreshing aromatics, along with tropical fruit flavors. We recommend using a London dry gin, which will have a bold enough flavor profile to come through in the finished drink.

1½ ounces aged rum

¾ ounce bourbon

½ ounce gin

1 ounce orange juice

1 ounce pineapple juice

1 ounce lime juice

½ ounce Orgeat (page 151)

¼ ounce Honey Syrup (page 150)

Combine all the ingredients in a shaker and fill with ice cubes. Shake vigorously for 20 to 30 seconds, until very cold. Strain the contents of the shaker into a rocks glass filled with crushed ice and serve.

happy buddha

MAKES 1

Guaranteed to put a smile on your face, the Happy Buddha is an easy-to-drink guava cocktail that is a delightful pink color. While most versions you'll find in tiki bars are served over crushed ice, we prefer to serve it without ice so that you can see the beautiful color of the drink as you sip it. That said, there are many ceramic Buddha tiki mugs out there and they are also an excellent choice when it comes to serving this cocktail.

1½ ounces white rum

2 ounces guava nectar

1 ounce Simple Syrup (page 150)

½ ounce ginger liqueur

Combine all the ingredients in a shaker and fill with ice cubes. Shake vigorously for 20 to 30 seconds, until very cold. Strain the contents of the shaker into a chilled coupe and serve.

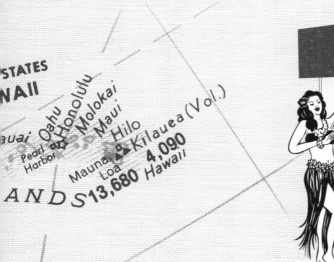

Where to Find Guava Nectar

Unless you live in the islands, you probably don't have access to fresh guava. There are several brands of guava nectar, available at most stores. Nectars that contain the most fresh guava juice and the least added sweeteners will give you the best results. You may have to taste test a few brands to find your favorite.

jungle bird

MAKES 1

The Jungle Bird is a cocktail for those who think that tiki drinks are always sweet—just to prove them wrong. This Campari-based drink not only has a vivid red color, but a distinct bitter note that comes both from the orange aperitif and from molasses-heavy dark Jamaican rum. It's rich and complex, with layers of flavor that will ensure you finish your drink so quickly that you'll need a second so that you can pick through them again.

1¼ ounces Campari

1 ounce dark Jamaican rum

1 ounce lime juice

½ ounce Cointreau

½ ounce Orgeat (page 151)

¼ ounce Spiced Simple Syrup (page 150)

Combine all the ingredients in a shaker and fill with ice cubes. Shake vigorously for 20 to 30 seconds, until very cold. Strain the contents of the shaker into a large rocks glass filled with crushed ice and serve.

mai tai

MAKES 1

Both Don the Beachcomber and Trader Vic laid claim to the invention of the Mai Tai in the early days of tiki. Don seemed to be the first one to use the name, but Trader Vic's version is the one that caught on and made the drink famous. His original recipe used a Jamaican rum, a seventeen-year-old J. Wray & Nephew, and the drink was such a hit that the supply of that rum was completely depleted. These days, the Mai Tai is usually made with a blend of aged Jamaican rum and unaged rhum agricole. The better rums you use, the better your Mai Tai will be—and you'll start to taste why this drink was such a huge hit.

1 ounce aged rum

1 ounce rhum agricole

¾ ounce lime juice

½ ounce orange curaçao

¼ ounce Orgeat (page 151)

½ ounce Simple Syrup (page 150)

Combine all the ingredients in a shaker and fill with ice cubes. Shake vigorously for 20 to 30 seconds, until very cold. Strain the contents of the shaker into a large rocks glass filled with crushed ice and serve.

missionary's downfall

MAKES 1

The Missionary's Downfall is another drink created by Don the Beachcomber, and the name really captures the irreverent spirit that made tiki culture so popular in the first place. This refreshing cocktail features a blend of white rum, pineapple, honey, and mint. We highly recommend using a white Demerara rum, which has a subtle fruitiness, to get the best results. As in the Aku Aku, the mint is shaken in with the rest of the cocktail ingredients and not strained out before serving, which gives the golden drink some intriguing flecks of color and ensures that it will remain bright and refreshing from start to finish.

1½ ounces white
Demerara rum

2 ounces pineapple juice

1 ounce lime juice

½ ounce Honey Syrup
(page 150)

4 to 5 fresh mint leaves

Combine all the ingredients, including the mint leaves, in a shaker and fill with crushed ice. Shake vigorously for 20 to 30 seconds, until very cold. Pour the contents of the shaker into a tall collins glass.

painkiller

MAKES 1

Pusser's rum is known as navy rum because it was originally distilled for members of the British Royal Navy, back in the days when sailors were giving a daily allotment of rum as part of their serving. It's a dark, rich rum with a subtle smokiness—and a Painkiller is always a good way to enjoy it. The drink has been Pusser's signature cocktail since the 1970s. The full-bodied rum stands up to the creamy coconut and pineapple flavors in the drink in a way that more subtle rums simply can't.

2 ounces Pusser's rum

4 ounces pineapple juice

1 ounce cream of coconut

1 ounce orange juice

Combine all the ingredients in a shaker and fill with ice cubes. Shake vigorously for 20 to 30 seconds, until very cold. Strain the contents of the shaker into a goblet filled with crushed ice and serve.

pineapple ti punch

MAKES 1

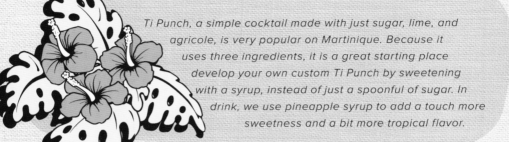

Ti Punch, a simple cocktail made with just sugar, lime, and agricole, is very popular on Martinique. Because it uses three ingredients, it is a great starting place develop your own custom Ti Punch by sweetening with a syrup, instead of just a spoonful of sugar. In drink, we use pineapple syrup to add a touch more sweetness and a bit more tropical flavor.

2 ounces rhum agricole

1 ounce Pineapple Syrup (page 151)

½ ounce lime juice

Combine all the ingredients in a rocks glass, fill with ice cubes, and stir to combine.

rum barrel

MAKES 1

The only thing better than a barrel full of rum is a Rum Barrel, which is a lot more practical if you only need one drink at a time. This cocktail is bright and citrusy, with a hint of spice to it. We recommend using navy-strength rum—which is bottled at a higher proof than other rums—because this drink needs a full bodied rum that can stand up to all the juice in it.

2 ounces aged rum

¾ ounce lime juice

¾ ounce orange juice

¾ ounce pineapple juice

¾ ounce passion fruit puree

¾ ounce Spiced Simple Syrup (page 150)

1 teaspoon Allspice Dram (page 153)

Combine all the ingredients in a shaker and fill with ice cubes. Shake vigorously for 20 to 30 seconds, until very cold. Strain the contents of the shaker into a highball glass filled with crushed ice and serve.

zombie

MAKES 1

Don the Beachcomber's Zombie might just be one of the most famous tiki drinks of all time—and one of the most mysterious. Not only did Don keep the original recipe a secret, but he tinkered with the ingredients over the years so that the drink kept evolving. This recipe sticks closely to the original—or what is said to be the original—with three different types of rum, a blend of citrus and spiced syrups, and a touch of absinthe. We recommend using a full-bodied Jamaican or Trinidadian rum as the aged rum in this cocktail.

1 ounce white rum

1½ ounces aged rum

½ ounce overproof rum

¾ ounce lime juice

½ ounce passion fruit puree

½ ounce Falernum
(page 152)

¼ ounce Spiced Simple
Syrup (page 150)

1 teaspoon grenadine

½ teaspoon absinthe

½ teaspoon Allspice Dram
(page 153)

Combine all the ingredients in a shaker and fill with ice cubes. Shake vigorously for 20 to 30 seconds, until very cold. Strain the contents of the shaker into a highball glass filled with crushed ice and serve.

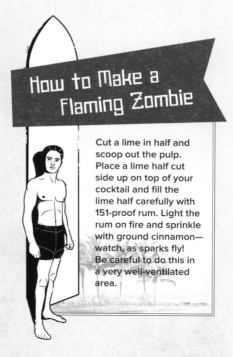

How to Make a Flaming Zombie

Cut a lime in half and scoop out the pulp. Place a lime half cut side up on top of your cocktail and fill the lime half carefully with 151-proof rum. Light the rum on fire and sprinkle with ground cinnamon— watch, as sparks fly! Be careful to do this in a very well-ventilated area.

rum crusta

MAKES 1

A crusta is a very old-fashioned style of cocktail, one is said to have been invented in New Orleans in the mid-1900s. The crusta is distinctive because it has a generously sugared rim and is garnished with a very, very large lemon twist. The original version featured brandy, but this rum variation is even more delicious because rum pairs so well with fresh lemon juice. This drink isn't particularly sweet because you get a taste of sugar every time you put your lips on the glass, so skip the straw when you go to serve it.

2 ounces aged rum

½ ounce Cointreau

¼ ounce *Luxardo* maraschino liqueur

½ ounce lemon juice

Combine all the ingredients in a shaker and fill with ice cubes. Shake vigorously for 20 to 30 seconds, until very cold. Strain the contents of the shaker into a small wineglass or rocks glass rimmed with sugar (see note). Garnish with a very wide lemon twist and serve.

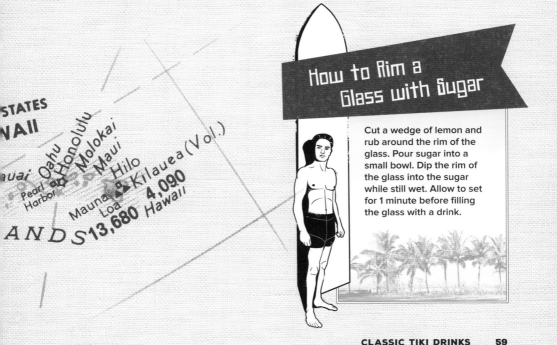

How to Rim a Glass with Sugar

Cut a wedge of lemon and rub around the rim of the glass. Pour sugar into a small bowl. Dip the rim of the glass into the sugar while still wet. Allow to set for 1 minute before filling the glass with a drink.

STATES
WAII

auai Oahu Honolulu
Pearl Molokai
Harbor Maui
Mauna Hilo
Loa Kilauea (Vol.)
4,090
ANDS 13,680 Hawaii

afterburner

MAKES 1

An afterburner provides an extra injection of fuel to jet engines to give them a boost of power when it is needed, and this cocktail is just the thing to give you an extra boost when you need it, too. It's a complex blend of rums and liqueurs, with just the right dash of citrus and spice to make it unforgettable. Unlike a jet plane, you probably won't reach supersonic speeds after getting wet with this Afterburner, but you will drink it down just as quickly as the jet burns fuel at maximum thrust.

1½ ounces dark rum

¾ ounce white rum

½ ounce Cointreau

½ ounce Falernum (page 152)

½ ounce lime juice

½ ounce Simple Syrup (page 150)

¼ ounce absinthe

1 dash of angostura bitters

Combine all the ingredients in a shaker and fill with ice cubes. Shake vigorously for 20 to 30 seconds, until very cold. Strain the contents of the shaker into a highball glass filled with crushed ice. Add a rocket ship (see note) and serve.

How to Make a Rocket Ship Garnish

Use a vegetable peeler to cut a long strip of lemon peel. Use the same peeler to cut a shorter strip of orange peel. Use a small knife to cut the larger strip of orange peel into a rocket ship shape, using a straw or a hole punch to add windows. Use a toothpick to pin the yellow trail to the orange rocket ship and insert, trail side down, along the edge of your glass.

banana manhattan

MAKES 1

Manhattan is a classic cocktail that is synonymous with sophistication. This tiki version of the drink takes a detour through the jungle before reaching the big city. It is made with an aged rum base and has just a touch of banana, which highlights the funky, fruity flavors in the rum without making the cocktail too sweet. We recommend using an aged Jamaican rum for this recipe, because it will naturally have those tropical flavors that the banana is there to emphasize.

1½ ounces aged rum

½ ounce Punt e Mes

½ ounce banana liqueur

2 dashes of angostura bitters

Combine all the ingredients in a shaker and fill with ice cubes. Shake vigorously for 20 to 30 seconds, until very cold. Double strain the contents of the shaker into a chilled martini glass and serve.

kona coffee swizzle

MAKES 1

The Kona Coffee Swizzle is an excellent choice when you need a little pick-me-up with your rum, just in case the zesty fruit juices used in most tiki drinks aren't enough to get you going. They say that a rum swizzle is Bermuda's national drink and, while this isn't exactly a traditional swizzle, thanks to the shot of coffee in it, we still recommend using a Bermuda rum if you have one on hand. If not, fruity Jamaican rums pair well with the Punt e Mes and create a cocktail that has a nice blend of sweet, fruity, and bitter flavors that is very refreshing on a hot summer night.

1 ounce aged rum

½ ounce dark rum

1 ounce strong coffee, chilled

½ ounce Punt e Mes

½ ounce Simple Syrup (page 150)

½ ounce orange juice

Combine all the ingredients in a highball glass and fill with crushed ice. Insert a swizzle stick and spin it vigorously between the palms of your hands until the ice begins to build up on the exterior of the glass. Garnish with orange peel. Serve.

creole daiquiri

MAKES 1

Rhum agricole is a great spirit to work with because of its complexity. Simple drinks, such as this easy-to-make daiquiri, are sometimes the best way to show it off. There is a touch of orange curaçao and a few dashes of orange bitters in this drink, just enough to add some summery sweetness to the rhum. Clément makes an orange liqueur called the Creole Shrub—where the inspiration for this drink name came from— that is even more delicious, if you have a chance to pick up a bottle.

2 ounces rhum agricole

¾ ounce lime juice

½ ounce Simple Syrup (page 150)

¼ ounce orange curaçao

2 dashes of orange bitters

Combine all the ingredients in a shaker and fill with ice cubes. Shake vigorously for 20 to 30 seconds, until very cold. Strain the contents of the shaker into a rocks glass filled with crushed ice and serve.

cunning monkey

MAKES 1

Banana is rarely the star in a cocktail, but it steals the show in this delightful drink. The combination of aged rum—we recommend using Jamaican rum—and banana liqueur is a surprisingly good one. The banana draws out the fruity notes of the rum and lets them stand apart from the darker molasses flavors. The result is a cocktail with a hint of caramelized banana flavor—which, incidentally, makes the perfect garnish.

1¼ ounces aged rum

1 ounce banana liqueur

¾ ounce Pineapple Syrup
(page 151)

½ ounce Falernum
(page 152)

1 (½-inch) slice caramelized
banana (see note)

Combine all the ingredients in a shaker and fill with ice cubes. Shake vigorously for 20 to 30 seconds, until very cold. Strain the contents of the shaker into a chilled martini glass, garnish with caramelized banana slice, and serve.

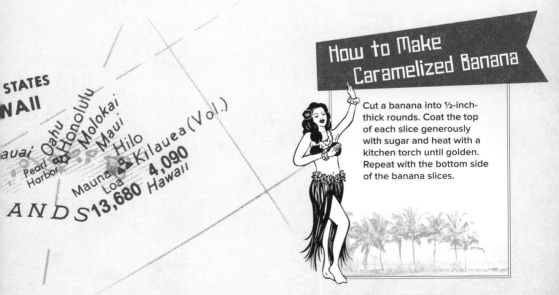

How to Make Caramelized Banana

Cut a banana into ½-inch-thick rounds. Coat the top of each slice generously with sugar and heat with a kitchen torch until golden. Repeat with the bottom side of the banana slices.

dead reckoning

MAKES 1

When you figure out where you are based on where you've been, you are using dead reckoning. This cocktail is a very modern tiki drink, with a rich array of herbal notes from both the aromatic gin and complex Green Chartreuse, but just the right touch of that tropical sweetness to remind you of all the great tropical drinks that came before this one.

1½ ounces gin

½ ounce Green Chartreuse

2 ounces pineapple juice

½ ounce lime juice

Combine all the ingredients in a shaker and fill with ice cubes. Shake vigorously for 20 to 30 seconds, until very cold. Strain the contents of the shaker into a chilled coupe. Garnish with a pineapple skull (see note) and serve.

How to Make a Pineapple Skull Garnish

Use a small skull-shaped cookie cutter *or* a knife to fashion a 2-inch piece of fresh pineapple into a skull. Use a small knife to add a teeth detail to the jawline of the skull. Add two whole cloves to the skull as eyes.

UNITED STATES
HAWAII

Necker Kauai Oahu Honolulu Molo
Nihoa   Pearl   Harbor

Maun

ISLANDS 13

far east

MAKES 1

One of the things that separate orgeat from other almond syrups is the orange blossom water used to flavor it. While it doesn't dominate the almond flavors, it adds an ethereal floral note to the finish that can be magical in cocktails. The Far East draws out those floral notes in a surprisingly creamy cocktail in which orange flower water and almond are allowed to take center stage.

2 ounces gin

1 ounce Pineapple Syrup (page 151)

1 ounce Orgeat (page 151)

¼ ounce lemon juice

2 dashes of angostura bitters

Combine all the ingredients in a shaker and fill with ice cubes. Shake vigorously for 20 to 30 seconds, until very cold. Strain the contents of the shaker into a chilled martini glass and serve.

skullduggery

MAKES 1

In this cocktail, overproof rum helps to temper the sweetness of the coconut and passion fruit that give the drink its creamy texture and brings your attention back to the dark rum at the base of the drink. This means you'll taste sweet coconut and molasses-kissed rum in each note. It also means that this concoction is dangerously easy to drink, as it strikes such a perfect balance between rum and fruit.

1½ ounces dark rum

¼ ounce overproof rum

3 ounces pineapple juice

1 ounce cream of coconut

1 ounce passion fruit puree

Combine all the ingredients in a shaker and fill with ice cubes. Shake vigorously for 20 to 30 seconds, until very cold. Strain the contents of the shaker into a Poco Grande filled with crushed ice. Garnish with an orange skull (see note) and serve.

How to Make an Orange Skull Garnish

Use a vegetable peeler to remove a 2-inch strip of peel from an orange peel. Use a small skull-shaped cookie cutter *or* a knife to fashion the orange peel strip into a skull. Use a hole punch or a straw to punch out the eyes and nose of the skull.

UNITED STATES
HAWAII

Necker Kauai Oahu Honolulu Molokai Maui
Nihoa   Pearl Harbor   Mauna Hi
                                                  Loa

ISLANDS 13,68

hawaiian queen bee

MAKES 1

Honey bees aren't native to Hawaii, but bees thrive in the warm, tropical climate, where they feed on sweet tropical nectars and pollinate all kinds of exotic ornamental and edible plants. Honey blends particularly well with rum, bringing out warm caramel notes in the spirit that sugar alone doesn't always add, while the rum tempers the sweetness of the honey. This drink is best made with an aged golden rum, which has more body than an unaged white rum does.

4 (1-inch) pieces pineapple

1½ ounces light rum

½ ounce overproof rum

1 ounce Honey Syrup (page 150)

¾ ounce lemon juice

Place the pineapple pieces in the bottom of a shaker and muddle to release their juice. Add all the remaining ingredients to the shaker and fill with ice cubes. Shake vigorously for 20 to 30 seconds, until very cold. Strain the contents of the shaker into a rocks glass rimmed with sugar (see note) and filled with crushed ice and serve.

How to Rim a Glass with Sugar

Rub a lemon wedge on the edge of the glass to moisten it. Sprinkle sugar onto a plate, then dip the rim of the glass in the sugar.

kahuna sour

MAKES 1

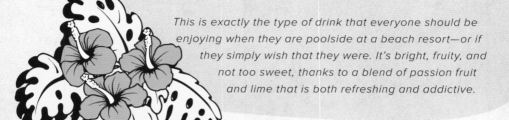

This is exactly the type of drink that everyone should be enjoying when they are poolside at a beach resort—or if they simply wish that they were. It's bright, fruity, and not too sweet, thanks to a blend of passion fruit and lime that is both refreshing and addictive.

2 ounces light rum

1 ounce lime juice

1 ounce passion fruit puree

½ ounce Falernum (page 152)

½ ounce Simple Syrup (page 150)

Combine all the ingredients in a shaker and fill with ice cubes. Shake vigorously for 20 to 30 seconds, until very cold. Strain the contents of the shaker into a rocks glass filled with crushed ice and serve.

UNITED STATES
HAWAII

Necker   Kauai   Oahu   Honolulu   Molokai   Maui
Nihoa   Pearl   Hilo
              Harbor   Mauna   Kilauea (Vol.)
                        Loa   4,090
ISLANDS 13,680 Hawaii

hurricane françois

MAKES 1

> This is a complex cocktail that isn't anything like what you'll be served wandering around New Orleans, where the original Hurricane cocktail comes from, but it is one hurricane you won't soon forget. The blush-colored cocktail has a slight earthiness from the combination of dark rum and rhum agricole, but what really stands out is the elegant floral notes from the blend of passion fruit and St-Germain liqueur.

1 ounce dark rum

1 ounce rhum agricole

1 ounce St-Germain liqueur

1 ounce passion fruit liqueur

½ ounce passion fruit puree

½ ounce lime juice

½ ounce Simple Syrup (page 150)

½ teaspoon grenadine

Combine all the ingredients in a shaker and fill with ice cubes. Shake vigorously for 20 to 30 seconds, until very cold. Strain the contents of the shaker into a hurricane glass filled with crushed ice and serve.

island hookup

MAKES 1

Spiced rum is not always a staple ingredient in a tiki bar because so many drinks call for the use of syrups and spice infusions that you don't necessarily need to start with a rum sweetened and spiced unto itself. But if you happen to have a bottle, there are still some great ways to use it. The Island Hookup relies on the extra sweetness of the spiced rum to help temper the bright citrus notes of lime and passion fruit and bring all these flavors together in one neat package.

1½ ounces spiced rum

¾ ounce lime juice

¾ ounce passion fruit puree

½ ounce Falernum (page 152)

¼ teaspoon *Luxardo* maraschino liqueur

Combine all the ingredients in a shaker and fill with ice cubes. Shake vigorously for 20 to 30 seconds, until very cold. Double strain the contents of the shaker into a chilled martini glass and serve.

island mai tai

MAKES 1

The Mai Tai might be one of the most recognized tiki drink names, but Trader Vic's original recipe isn't as popular as the fruitier, pineapple-heavy version that is much more commonly seen at tropical resorts. We like them both, and even tiki purists will admit it is hard to resist this particular version, with its perfect combination of sweet pineapple juice and molasses-forward black strap rum. Don't skip the float on top of this drink, as it is what takes it from being a good cocktail to being an unforgettable one.

1 ounce white rum

1 ounce triple sec

2 ounces orange juice

2 ounces pineapple juice

1 ounce lime juice

1 ounce Simple Syrup (page 150)

½ ounce Cruzan Black Strap Rum

Combine all the ingredients except the black strap rum in a shaker and fill with ice cubes. Shake vigorously for 20 to 30 seconds, until very cold. Strain the contents of the shaker into a Poco Grande glass filled with crushed ice. Float the black strap rum on top of the cocktail and serve.

jamaican milk punch

MAKES 1

Milk punch is one of the oldest mixed drinks, enjoyed by drinkers since colonial times. Milk punch may not be as fashionable as it once was, but one sip of this coconut milk punch will put you back on the milk punch bandwagon. The drink is rich and creamy, with a perfect sweetness that makes each sip go down very easily. If you have a machete and a few coconuts on hand, you can serve this punch in a coconut shell to give it a little extra tiki style.

1½ ounces aged
Jamaican rum

½ ounce overproof rum

2 ounces cream of coconut

2 ounces whole milk

1 teaspoon Simple Syrup
(page 150)

Combine all the ingredients in a shaker and fill with ice cubes. Shake vigorously for 20 to 30 seconds, until very cold. Strain the contents of the shaker into a large rocks glass filled with crushed ice and serve.

low tide

MAKES 1

Low tide is the best time to head down to the beach if you're a beachcombing type because that is when you will get easy access to a variety of shells and vibrantly colored sea creatures that are usually hidden from view. This cocktail is may be boldly colored, but the tastes of lime, melon, and spice are surprisingly subtle, so you'll have many layers of flavor to discover as you sip.

1½ ounces white rum

¾ ounce Midori melon liqueur

¼ ounce Allspice Dram (page 152)

½ ounce triple sec

½ ounce lime juice

¼ ounce Spiced Simple Syrup (page 150)

Combine all the ingredients in a shaker and fill with ice cubes. Shake vigorously for 20 to 30 seconds, until very cold. Strain the contents of the shaker into a rocks glass filled with crushed ice and serve.

molokai mule

MAKES 1

Bucks and mules are old-fashioned names for drinks made with citrus and ginger beer, along with a generous pour of spirits. The best know is the Moscow Mule, which uses vodka as its base spirit. This Molokai Mule has a decidedly more tropical flair, with just the right amount of pineapple sweetness to contrast with the allspice and ginger that dominate the drink. Ginger beer can dominate rums that are too mild, so an aged rum is a good choice for this recipe.

1½ ounces aged rum

¾ ounce Pineapple Syrup (page 151)

¼ ounce Allspice Dram (page 153)

3 to 4 ounces ginger beer

Combine the rum, pineapple syrup, and allspice dram in a large rocks glass or a copper mug. Fill with ice and top with ginger beer, then serve.

baja tiki

MAKES 1

Part of the fun of visiting a tiki bar is that you get to feel as if you're on vacation without ever leaving your home town. This cocktail puts a tiki twist on a Mexican classic, the margarita, by combining rum and tequila in one drink. You will be able to taste the sweetness of the rum and the vegetal agave flavor of the tequila, and it will taste both familiar and exotic. We finished this off by rimming the glass with a blend of sugar and Tajin, a spicy Mexican seasoning that is often paired with fruit to accentuate its sweetness.

1 ounce reposado tequila

1 ounce light rum

½ ounce triple sec

1 ounce pineapple juice

½ ounce lime juice

½ ounce Orgeat (page 151)

1 teaspoon *Luxardo* maraschino liqueur

Tajin seasoning–sugar mixture (see note)

Combine all the ingredients in a shaker and fill with ice cubes. Shake vigorously for 20 to 30 seconds, until very cold. Strain the contents of the shaker into a goblet rimmed with Tajin seasoning–sugar mixture and filled with crushed ice, then serve.

How to Rim a Glass with the Taijin Seasoning– Sugar Mixture

Rub a lime wedge on the edge of the glass to moisten it. Combine equal parts sugar and Tajin seasoning mixture on a plate or in a shallow bowl, then dip the rim of the glass into the mixture.

nutty pirate

MAKES 1

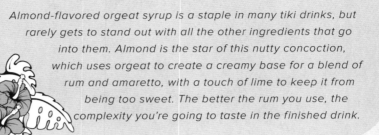

Almond-flavored orgeat syrup is a staple in many tiki drinks, but rarely gets to stand out with all the other ingredients that go into them. Almond is the star of this nutty concoction, which uses orgeat to create a creamy base for a blend of rum and amaretto, with a touch of lime to keep it from being too sweet. The better the rum you use, the complexity you're going to taste in the finished drink.

2 ounces aged rum

¼ ounce amaretto

¼ ounce apricot brandy

¾ ounce lime juice

¼ ounce Orgeat (page 151)

¼ ounce Spiced Simple Syrup (page 150)

Combine all the ingredients in a shaker and fill with ice cubes. Shake vigorously for 20 to 30 seconds, until very cold. Strain the contents of the shaker into a large rocks glass filled with crushed ice and serve.

UNITED STATES
HAWAII

Necker Kauai Oahu Honolulu Molokai
Nihoa   Pearl on Maui Hilo
                Harbor   Mauna Kilauea (Vol.)
                          Loa 13,680 4,090 Hawaii

I S L A N D S

pineapple bramble

MAKES 1

*Layers of fruit flavors are always welcome in tiki drinks, and this juicy
Pineapple Bramble is bursting with them. The key ingredient in a bramble
is a blackberry liqueur, known as Crème de Mûre, which gives the cocktail
a beautiful purple color and a rich berry flavor. The liqueur isn't a common
bar ingredient, but it is delicious and has a much longer shelf life than fresh
berries do, allowing you to enjoy this summery cocktail all year round.*

4 (1-inch) pieces pineapple

2 ounces aged rum

¾ ounce lemon juice

½ ounce Simple Syrup
(page 150)

½ ounce blackberry liqueur

Place the pineapple pieces in the bottom of a shaker and
muddle to release their juice. Add the rum, lemon juice, and
simple syrup to the shaker and fill with ice cubes. Shake
vigorously for 20 to 30 seconds, until very cold. Strain the
contents of the shaker into a rocks glass rimmed with sugar
and filled with crushed ice. Drizzle in the blackberry liqueur
and serve.

pineapple caipirinha

MAKES 1

Caipirinha is Brazil's version of the daiquiri, a simple and addicting drink that is ubiquitous at every bar—and at every party—in the country. It's made with cachaça, a spirit made with fresh sugarcane that is similar to rum and an ingredient that would have undoubtedly been as much of a tiki staple as Jamaican, Puerto Rican, and other rums if only the original tiki pioneers had been able to get their hands on some. You won't find this drink on any classic tiki menus, but it would fit right in with those flavors.

2 ounces cachaça

1 ounce Pineapple Syrup (page 151)

½ ounce Simple Syrup (page 150)

½ lime, cut into thirds

2 (1-inch) pieces pineapple

Combine the lime and pineapple in the bottom of a rocks glass with the simple syrup and muddle to release their juices. Add the cachaça and pineapple syrup, then fill the glass with ice cubes and stir to combine. Serve.

sherry longboard

MAKES 1

Not all tiki drinks have a long, complicated ingredient list and one reason is that they often use ingredients that have a complex flavor on their own. Sherry, a Spanish fortified wine, is a very complex ingredient—particularly if you are dealing with a rich, aged Amontillado sherry. This Sherry Longboard is easy to drink in hot weather and has a nice blend of pineapple and honey notes without being overly sweet.

2 ounces Amontillado sherry

2 ounces pineapple juice

1 ounce Simple Syrup (page 150)

Fill a collins glass with crushed ice and pour the ingredients over the ice. Stir to combine and serve.

puffer fish

MAKES 1

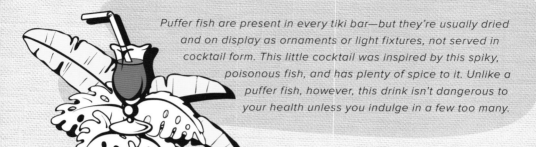

Puffer fish are present in every tiki bar—but they're usually dried and on display as ornaments or light fixtures, not served in cocktail form. This little cocktail was inspired by this spiky, poisonous fish, and has plenty of spice to it. Unlike a puffer fish, however, this drink isn't dangerous to your health unless you indulge in a few too many.

2 ounces aged rum

¼ ounce dark rum

½ ounce lime juice

½ ounce Allspice Dram
(page 153)

¼ ounce Simple Syrup
(page 150)

2 to 3 ounces ginger beer

Combine all the ingredients except the ginger beer in a shaker and fill with ice cubes. Shake vigorously for 20 to 30 seconds, until very cold. Strain the contents of the shaker into a large rocks glass filled with crushed ice. Top with the ginger beer and serve.

UNITED STATES
HAWAII

Necker Kauai Oahu Honolulu Molokai
Nihoa Pearl Maui Hilo
Harbor Mauna Kilauea
Loa 4,090
ISLANDS 13,680 Hawaii

shipwreck daiquiri

MAKES 1

A classic daiquiri is made with rum, lime and simple syrup. It is easy to take this basic drink to a whole new level by switching up some of the ingredients for more complex ones. This daiquiri is made with an aged navy-strength rum and is sweetened with apricot brandy to give it both body and sweetness. A touch of banana helps some of the tropical notes in the rum really shine.

1½ ounces aged rum

¾ ounce apricot brandy

½ ounce lime juice

1 teaspoon banana liqueur

Flaming orange peel (see note)

Combine all the ingredients, except the orange peel, in a shaker and fill with ice cubes. Shake vigorously for 20 to 30 seconds, until very cold. Strain the contents of the shaker into a chilled coupe glass. Garnish with a flaming orange peel and serve.

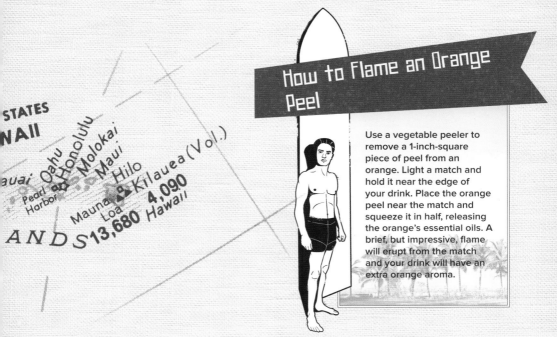

How to Flame an Orange Peel

Use a vegetable peeler to remove a 1-inch-square piece of peel from an orange. Light a match and hold it near the edge of your drink. Place the orange peel near the match and squeeze it in half, releasing the orange's essential oils. A brief, but impressive, flame will erupt from the match and your drink will have an extra orange aroma.

siren's song

MAKES 1

The songs of sirens are said to have lured many sailors into shipwrecks in rocky, treacherous waters. Their lovely voices were simply irresistible—as were their looks, according to the legends that surround them. Like those sirens, this beguiling pink cocktail looks harmless, but it actually has a little bit of a bite to it. It has a soft floral flavor from guava juice and a generous splash of lemon juice to tame that tropical guava flavor and keep the cocktail bright and balanced.

1½ ounces light rum

¼ ounce dark rum

½ ounce triple sec

1 ounce guava nectar

¾ ounce lemon juice

½ ounce Honey Syrup (page 150)

2 to 4 ounces ginger beer

Combine all the ingredients except the ginger beer in a shaker and fill with ice cubes. Shake vigorously for 20 to 30 seconds, until very cold. Strain the contents of the shaker into a large rocks glass filled with crushed ice. Fill the glass to the top with ginger beer and serve.

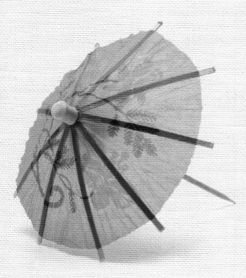

spiced park swizzle

MAKES 1

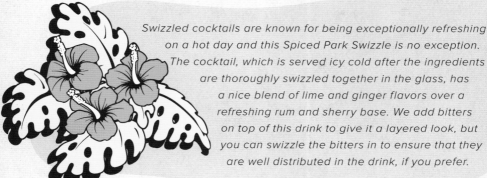

Swizzled cocktails are known for being exceptionally refreshing on a hot day and this Spiced Park Swizzle is no exception. The cocktail, which is served icy cold after the ingredients are thoroughly swizzled together in the glass, has a nice blend of lime and ginger flavors over a refreshing rum and sherry base. We add bitters on top of this drink to give it a layered look, but you can swizzle the bitters in to ensure that they are well distributed in the drink, if you prefer.

1 ounce rhum agricole

1 ounce Amontillado sherry

½ ounce Falernum (page 152)

½ ounce ginger liqueur

1 ounce lime juice

¼ ounce Simple Syrup (page 150)

5 dashes of angostura bitters

Combine all the ingredients, except the bitters, in a highball glass and fill with crushed ice. Insert a swizzle stick and spin it vigorously between the palms of your hands until the ice begins to build up on the exterior of the glass. Shake the bitters on top to create a layered look. Serve.

UNITED STATES
HAWAII

Necker Kauai Oahu Honolulu Molokai Maui Hilo
Nihoa Pearl Harbor Mauna Loa Kilauea (Vol.) 4,090
ISLANDS 13,680 Hawaii

spouting horn

MAKES 1

Spouting Horn is a spectacular, natural blowhole on Kauai where you can watch huge plumes of seawater jet into the air as the tide comes in and out. This cocktail won't spurt out of the glass, but it does have plenty of bubbles to give it some effervescence of its own. We recommend using Squirt soda for this drink because it has a strong grapefruit flavor and a nice sweetness; however, other grapefruit sodas will also turn out a wonderful version of this cocktail.

2 ounces aged rum

½ ounce Spiced Simple Syrup (page 150)

¼ ounce Orgeat (page 151)

Grapefruit soda

Combine the rum, spiced simple syrup, and orgeat in a collins glass and fill with crushed ice. Top with grapefruit soda, then serve.

death in paradise

MAKES 1

It can be hard to take a blue cocktail seriously—after all, there aren't even many blue foods—but Death in Paradise is a good place to start. It is a perfectly balanced tropical punch that is definitely not for kids. This cocktail starts with earthy rhum agricole and complements it with layers of ginger, orange, lime, and a hint of spice. Honey syrup lends just the right sweetness to bring all the flavors together.

2 ounces rhum agricole

¾ ounce ginger liqueur

½ ounce lime juice

½ ounce blue curaçao

½ ounce Honey Syrup
(page 150)

¼ ounce Falernum
(page 152)

Combine all the ingredients in a shaker and fill with ice cubes. Shake vigorously for 20 to 30 seconds, until very cold. Strain the contents of the shaker into a highball glass filled with crushed ice and serve.

tennessee tai

MAKES 1

This version of a Mai Tai is one we first encountered in a bar in Nashville, where they used locally made Tennessee whiskey in all kinds of new ways. It is a great spin on a traditional Mai Tai, as the whiskey adds some nice oak and vanilla notes to the drink, while the spiced rum adds a little sweetness to further draw that vanilla out of the whiskey. Trader Vic would probably approve.

1 ounce spiced rum

1 ounce Tennessee whiskey

1 ounce lime juice

½ ounce Cointreau

¼ ounce Orgeat (page 151)

¼ ounce Simple Syrup
(page 150)

Combine all the ingredients in a shaker and fill with ice cubes. Shake vigorously for 20 to 30 seconds, until very cold. Strain the contents of the shaker into a highball glass filled with crushed ice and serve.

tahitienne

MAKES 1

*One of the most refreshing tropical drinks you can have—besides a tiki
drink, of course—is coconut water, and there is no better way to enjoy it
than straight out of a fresh coconut. The light, creamy Tahitienne uses both
coconut water and coconut cream for a dreamy cocktail that will make you
think you're right on an island beach, with a freshly picked coconut in hand.*

1½ ounces white rum

2 ounces coconut water

1 ounce cream of coconut

¼ ounce orange curaçao

Combine all the ingredients in a shaker and fill with ice cubes.
Shake vigorously for 20 to 30 seconds, until very cold. Strain
the contents of the shaker into a chilled coupe glass and
serve.

malay mist

MAKES 1

Not every tiki drink is rum based. This cocktail uses gin because it is herbaceous enough to stand out against the sweet coconut and pineapple and give the drink a really refreshing quality. At the same time, those sweeter ingredients tone down the juniper flavors in the gin—and we recommend sticking with a classic London Dry in this recipe—and create a drink that everyone can enjoy.

1½ ounces gin

1 ounce cream of coconut

1 ounce lime juice

1 ounce pineapple juice

1 teaspoon Simple Syrup (page 150)

Combine all the ingredients in a shaker and fill with ice cubes. Shake vigorously for 20 to 30 seconds, until very cold. Strain the contents of the shaker into a large rocks glass filled with crushed ice and serve.

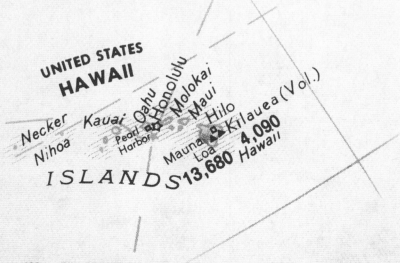

hula skirt

MAKES 1

The bold, bright color of this cocktail makes it stand out in a crowd, but the drink isn't as sweet as it looks. Most of that vibrant color comes from Campari, which has a bitter orange flavor that is quite unexpected when you take your first sip. The orange blends well with the lime and spice flavors that are also in this cocktail, making for a drink that is absolutely intriguing from the first sip to the last.

2 ounces aged rum

¼ ounce lime juice

¼ ounce Campari

½ ounce Falernum (page 152)

1 teaspoon grenadine

Combine all the ingredients in a shaker and fill with ice cubes. Shake vigorously for 20 to 30 seconds, until very cold. Strain the contents of the shaker into a chilled coupe glass. Garnish with a hula skirt (see note) and serve.

How to Make a Hula Skirt Garnish

Cut a lime in half, then cut a small opening in the end of one half and scoop out the pulp. Using a pair of scissors, cut vertical slits all around the lime shell, being careful not to cut all the way through the lime shell. Place on the rim of the glass as a garnish.

outrigger

MAKES 1

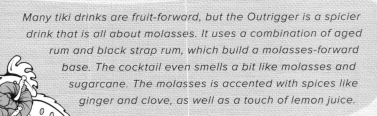

Many tiki drinks are fruit-forward, but the Outrigger is a spicier drink that is all about molasses. It uses a combination of aged rum and black strap rum, which build a molasses-forward base. The cocktail even smells a bit like molasses and sugarcane. The molasses is accented with spices like ginger and clove, as well as a touch of lemon juice.

¾ ounce aged rum

¾ ounce Cruzan Black Strap Rum

½ ounce Domaine de Canton liqueur

½ ounce lemon juice

½ ounce Falernum (page 152)

Combine all the ingredients in a shaker and fill with ice cubes. Shake vigorously for 20 to 30 seconds, until very cold. Strain the contents of the shaker into a rocks glass filled with crushed ice and serve.

queen anne's revenge

MAKES 1

Queen Anne's Revenge is the name of Blackbeard's pirate ship, captured from the English by the French and from the French by the famous pirate captain. The ship served as a pirate vessel for only a year, but that year was infamous. Like the ship, this cocktail has a French twist to it in the form of elderflower liqueur. It lends a lovely floral sweetness to the very refreshing drink, which is a good choice on a hot summer evening when you wish you were feeling a cool sea breeze.

2 ounce aged rum

1 ounce St-Germain liqueur

½ ounce lime juice

½ ounce Falernum (page 152)

10 to 12 fresh mint leaves

Combine all the ingredients—including the mint leaves—in a shaker and fill with ice cubes. Shake vigorously for 20 to 30 seconds, until very cold. Double strain the contents of the shaker into a rocks glass filled with crushed ice. Slap the mint in the palm of your hand (see note), then garnish the drink with the mint and serve.

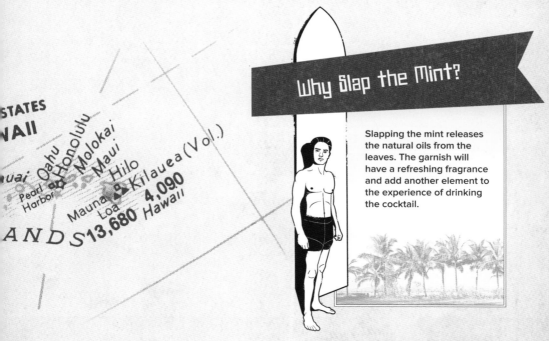

Why Slap the Mint?

Slapping the mint releases the natural oils from the leaves. The garnish will have a refreshing fragrance and add another element to the experience of drinking the cocktail.

rob's mistake

One of the best known tiki bars in Los Angeles is Tiki Ti, which has been owned and operated by the same family since it opened in 1961. Its best-selling drink is Ray's Mistake, named after founder Ray Buhen. Like many tiki drinks, the recipe for Ray's Mistake is a closely guarded secret and contains so many ingredients that it is not easy to replicate at home. This drink is inspired by the Tiki Ti original and, while it's not an exact replica of that cocktail, it is one mistake well worth making.

ounce light rum

1 ounce London dry gin

1 ounce lime juice

1 ounce passion fruit puree

½ ounce Frangelico

½ ounce Pineapple Syrup (page 151)

1 teaspoon grenadine

½ ounce dark rum

Combine all the ingredients, except the dark rum, in a shaker and fill with ice cubes. Shake vigorously for 20 to 30 seconds, until very cold. Strain the contents of the shaker into a highball glass filled with crushed ice. Float the dark rum on top and serve.

south seas sling

MAKES 1

The Singapore Sling was invented at the Raffles Hotel in Singapore in 1915 and is often cited as a tiki drink, though the cocktail predates the first tiki bars by more than a decade. The drink has more variations than you can shake a stick at and many are very delicious. This is our own twist on that classic cocktail. It's a gin-based drink that has a lot of complexity, thanks to a surprising blend of different liqueurs.

1½ ounces London dry gin

1 ounce Cherry Heering

1 ounce lime juice

½ ounce brandy

½ ounce apricot brandy

½ ounce Spiced Simple Syrup (page 150)

Combine all the ingredients in a shaker and fill with ice cubes. Shake vigorously for 20 to 30 seconds, until very cold. Strain the contents of the shaker into a highball glass filled with crushed ice.

cachaça batida

MAKES 1

Batidas are a type of Brazilian cocktail that is typically made with fresh fruit juices and generous amount of cachaça. Served on the rocks or blended, they're a great way to beat the Brazilian heat in the summer. This blended drink uses coconut and sweetened condensed milk for an exceptionally creamy concoction. The ingredients sound sweet on their own, but that sweetness is tempered by the ice by the time the cocktail is blended up. These are great for a party, since it is easy to make—and easy to drink—a big batch.

2 ounces cachaça

2 ounces cream of coconut

2 ounces sweetened condensed milk

½ ounce Simple Syrup (page 150)

5 ounces ice

Combine all the ingredients in a blender. Blend at low speed for several seconds to crush the ice, then blend at high speed until the drink is smooth. Serve in a chilled Poco Grande.

piña colada

MAKES 1

A Piña Colada is one of the best-known blended tropical drinks for a reason: it is absolutely delicious. Our secret is to use pineapple chunks in the drink, which gives it a much fresher flavor than you'll find in most versions. Fresh pineapple is always our first choice, since having a whole pineapple on hand also means we will have plenty of fruit around for garnish; however canned pineapple rings will work just as well.

2 ounces white rum

2 ounces pineapple juice

2 ounces cream of coconut

4 (1-inch) pieces pineapple

5 to 6 ounces ice

Combine all the ingredients in a blender. Blend at low speed for several seconds to crush the ice, then blend at high speed until the drink is smooth. Serve in a chilled goblet or Poco Grande.

lava flow

MAKES 1

Piña colada fans might find that they become Lava Flow converts after tasting this tropical cocktail. It starts with a sweetened strawberry puree, placed at the base of a large glass. A blended piña colada is poured over the puree, causing the bright red puree to swirl up and into the off-white blended drink and giving it the look of a lava flow! Be sure to use a clear glass when making these, as seeing the colors through the sides of the glass is part of the fun of serving them!

1 recipe Piña Colada (page 136)

1½ ounces strawberry puree (see note)

Prepare the piña colada. Place the strawberry puree at the base of a hurricane glass, then pour the piña colada mixture over the top, allowing the liquids to swirl together. Serve.

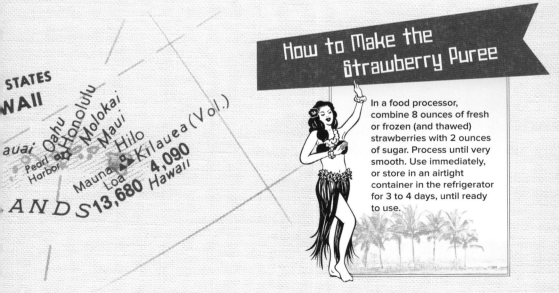

How to Make the Strawberry Puree

In a food processor, combine 8 ounces of fresh or frozen (and thawed) strawberries with 2 ounces of sugar. Process until very smooth. Use immediately, or store in an airtight container in the refrigerator for 3 to 4 days, until ready to use.

hula kula

MAKES 1

Passion fruit is one of our favorite fruits to use in tiki drinks and this one has it in spades, with both passion fruit puree and passion fruit liqueur in the drink. The secret to this drink's success is the egg white that is blended right in with the rest of the ingredients. It gives the Hula Kula a surprisingly airy yet creamy texture. You can use a pasteurized-in-shell egg or replace the whole egg white with bottled egg whites, which also come pasteurized. The bottled egg whites are easier to use if you're blending these for a crowd.

1½ ounces aged rum

1 ounce passion fruit liqueur

3 ounces passion fruit puree

1 ounce Simple Syrup
(page 150)

½ ounce lemon juice

1 large egg white

6 ounces ice

Combine all the ingredients in a blender. Blend at low speed for several seconds to crush the ice, then blend at high until the drink is smooth. Serve in a chilled goblet or rocks glass.

groggaccino

MAKES 1

Blended coffee drinks are delicious, and they are even more delicious when you spike them with a little bit of rum. This particular coffee drink is much more appropriate for dessert than for breakfast, even though it has enough coffee to give you a nice boost of energy, since it is also laced with aged rum and Kahlúa. Whipped cream isn't an ingredient in our tiki bar, but free to indulge and put a dollop on top of your Groggaccino after you whip one up.

1 ounce aged rum

1 ounce Kahlúa

½ ounce crème de cacao

1 ounce cream of coconut

1 ounce milk

½ ounce Spiced Simple Syrup (page 150)

5 to 6 ounces ice

½ ounce Cruzan Black Strap Rum

1 oz strong coffee, chilled

Combine all the ingredients, except the black strap rum, in a blender. Blend at low speed for several seconds to crush the ice, then blend at high speed until the drink is smooth. Pour into a chilled goblet or Poco Grande and float the black strap rum on top before serving.

blue lagoon punch

SERVES 2 TO 3

Tiki drinks are always more fun when they're shared with friends and tropical punches are made for sharing. This Blue Lagoon Punch is actually a simple pineapple and rum punch that has a dramatic azure blue color that makes you want to plunge a straw right in and drink it down. It is best when served in a big bowl—even if you don't yet have a dedicated tiki bowl—and shared with three or four people

2 ounces white rum

1 ounce overproof rum

1 ounce lime juice

1 ounce Orgeat (page 151)

½ ounce blue curaçao

3 ounces pineapple juice

1 ounce Pineapple Syrup
(page 151)

In a medium-size bowl, stir together all the ingredients. Pour into a tiki bowl or punch bowl and fill with crushed ice. Serve immediately.

scorpion bowl

SERVES 2 TO 3

The Scorpion Bowl is one of those drinks that you see on many tiki menus, but it rarely tastes the same way twice, even though the original concoction has been around for decades. Our version sticks to a classic recipe, made with rum and brandy, as well as a combination of orange and lemon juice. We always add orange bitters to intensify the orange flavor without watering the drink down, and highly recommend topping it off with a generous pour of sparkling wine. This version serves two, but it can easily be doubled if you have more friends to share it with.

2 ounces white rum

1 ounce brandy

2 ounces orange juice

1 ounce lemon juice

½ ounce Orgeat (page 151)

4 to 5 dashes of orange bitters

Sparkling wine or Moscato

In a large bowl, stir together all the ingredients, except the sparkling wine. Pour into a tiki bowl or punch bowl and fill with crushed ice. Top with sparkling wine. Serve immediately.

UNITED STATES
HAWAII

Necker Kauai Oahu Honolulu Molokai
Nihoa   Pearl on Maui Hilo
               Harbor   Mauna ▲ Kilauea (Vol.)
                           Loa 4,090
ISLANDS 13,680 Hawaii

allspice dram

MAKES ABOUT 2 CUPS

Allspice dram, also known as pimento dram, is a strongly flavored liqueur that is infused with peppery allspice berries. A small quantity goes a long way, and it adds a fantastic spice to every drink it appears in. You can use just about any rum in this recipe, as the allspice is so potent, and we recommend using up something inexpensive. This dram tastes a bit better after it sits for a few days, so plan ahead to make it in advance.

8 ounces rum, any kind

8 ounces Simple Syrup (page 150)

¼ cup allspice berries, lightly crushed

1½ teaspoons vanilla extract

In a sealable bottle or other airtight container, combine all the ingredients. Shake to combine, then allow to steep for 2 to 4 days in a cool, dark place, agitating a few times each day.

Strain out the allspice by pouring the syrup through a fine-mesh sieve or a coffee filter and transfer the syrup to a clean, airtight container.

The syrup can be stored at room temperature and will keep almost indefinitely in a cool, dry place.

INDEX